ON CHESTNUTS

ON CHESTNUTS

THE TREES AND THEIR SEEDS

Ria Loohuizen

with a foreword by
Jill Norman

Drawings by Rein Dool

PROSPECT BOOKS
2006

First published in Great Britain in 2006 by Prospect Books, Allaleigh House, Blackawton, Totnes, Devon TQ9 7DL.

This book, entitled *Van de kastanje*, was first published in the Netherlands by Uitgeverij Atlas, Amsterdam in 2002. The present translation is by the author.

British Library Cataloguing in Publication Data:
A catalogue entry for this book is available from the British Library.

ISBN 1-903018-32-3
Typeset by Tom Jaine.
Printed in Great Britain at the Cromwell Press, Trowbridge, Wiltshire.

Contents

Foreword

My childhood memories of chestnuts are of roasting them in front of the fire, precariously perched on long forks, and the patience (and burned fingers) needed to roast them evenly on all sides. The adults drank sherry with theirs, we children were given cocoa. I remember the pleasure of those evenings when I buy chestnuts from a street vendor in autumn, once more burning my fingers to get them out of the shell.

Several ancient chestnut trees survive in Britain; the best known is the huge sprawling tree at Tortworth in Gloucestershire. John Evelyn (1620–1706) described it as the 'great chestnut' and claimed that it had been a boundary marker in the 12th century. Today, branches from the twisted trunk lie on the ground and have rooted to become trees in their own right, with new trunks and branches thrusting out to create a small woodland.

Evelyn lamented the fact that chestnuts were prized by generations of southern Europeans, but considered only fit for pigs in Britain. In the appendix to *Acetaria* he gives instructions for serving roasted and shelled chestnuts with orange juice, sugar and claret. 'Delicacies for princes' and 'lusty food for rusticks' is how he described them.

Native to southern Europe, the chestnut has long been widely cultivated in Spain, France and Italy for its wood – for furniture and building, for barrels for wine and vinegar (chestnut barrels are still used in the production of balsamic vinegar) – and for its fruit. Once an essential staple, these regions offer excellent recipes for chestnuts combined with other seasonal foods such as mushrooms, pumpkin and quince. The chestnut is celebrated at village fêtes and grander festivals, such as the Châtaigneraie held every October at Mourjou in central France.

The Japanese are also enthusiastic chestnut eaters. In a Japanese restaurant recently I was served a candied chestnut as garnish to a delicate piece of black cod. Chestnut rice is a popular autumn dish, and chestnuts are steamed with fish and made into many desserts, including a Japanese version of marrons glacés.

In the mid-20th century, Hilda Leyel still considered that chestnuts were not appreciated in England as they should be, and in *The Gentle Art of Cookery* devoted a chapter of enticing, if sometimes sketchy, recipes to them. The fine and carefully written recipes in *On Chestnuts* should encourage us to extend our repertoire beyond stuffing for a bird or a dish of Brussels sprouts and chestnuts to accompany one. Ria Loohuizen offers many tempting, elegant main dishes and desserts as well as substantial soups and breads, together with stimulating reading about sweet and horse chestnuts in their historical and cultural context.

Jill Norman

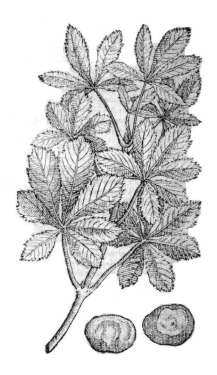

Castanea equina, *from Carolus Clusius,* Rariorum plantarum historia
(ca. *1585).*

I *The horse chestnut,*
Aesculus hippocastanum

Marron d'Inde – French
Castagno – Italian
Castaño de Indias – Spanish
Kastanie – German
Kasztan – Polish

Biology teacher

On his insistence
I became a father
in my tenth year
when after a tense wait
a chestnut kept in water
released a yellow shoot
and everything around
burst into song.

ZBIGNIEW HERBERT

People who are surrounded by trees or are in the habit of observing them, may become aware that trees have something that most wild animals don't have, something they have in common with people: individuality.

The horse chestnut is a tree which stimulates the sense of touch – from the early spring, when the fat sticky buds are about to burst open, to the autumn, when the prickly bolsters appear that turn out to contain surprisingly smooth, shiny brown treasures. Chestnut: a nut in a chest that you can't help picking up and putting in your pocket, like a pretty pebble, only much warmer in the hand.

The horse chestnut – a tree of stately appearance, especially in a park landscape – can reach a height of 20 to 35 metres. It is a tree with a strong personality which can reach a very old age, though not quite as old as the sweet chestnut, to which it is not related.

The horse chestnut has its origins in the region of the Himalayas and was brought to Europe from the Middle East in the 16th century by the inspired Flemish diplomat, linguist, writer and amateur botanist Ghislain de Busbeck (1522–1592), to whom we also owe the tulip and the lilac. The first example reached the Netherlands in 1608 and was planted in the Botanical Gardens of Leyden University by the Flemish botanist Carolus Clusius (1526–1609), who went on many field excursions throughout Europe, especially in the Alps, the Balkans, Austria and Hungary. Around 1581 he received horse chestnut seeds from one of Busbeck's successors as ambassador in Constantinople. He managed to grow a small plant, but as the tree doesn't bloom until it is mature, its blossom remained a mystery to him for years. He made drawings for his book *Rariorem plantarum historia*, from which in turn woodcuts were made in Antwerp – now preserved in the Museum Plantin-Moretus. He found the time to devote to *Rariorem*, one of the earliest floras, after a severe fall confined him to his quarters.

GROWTH AND HABITAT

Sedge-warblers
Clearer than any goddess or man's daughter,
And harkened while it combed the dark green hair
And shook the millions of the blossoms white
Of water-crowfoot, and curdled to one sheet
The flowers fallen from the chestnuts in the park
Far off.

EDWARD THOMAS

My front window affords a view of one of the oldest chestnut trees in Amsterdam, planted in 1895. In winter, when all the leaves are gone, it reveals its characteristic spreading shape: the lower boughs droop, their twigs point upward; throughout the winter the fat, sticky buds are swelling imperceptibly and when they open, usually in May, they unfold light green leaves protected by tiny hairs.

The hand-shaped leaves with their long stems are composed of five or seven separate, feather-shaped leaves, ten to twenty centimetres in length, dark green on top, slightly yellow and hairy underneath. The bark of the trunk is smooth at first, later it partially peels off.

The blooming of the horse chestnut (sometimes only after thirty years) is a festive occasion: one tree may contain 50,000 white 'candles'. The flowers emerge on upright spikes at the end of the twigs and each have both stamens and pistil; the flowers pollinated by insects show a little red stain on their petals. There is also a variety of horse chestnut that has pink or red blossoms.

After the blossoms, the little green 'chests' appear, first the size of a marble, until in the autumn the spiky cases have become as large as ping-pong balls, bursting open to allow the seeds, with the typical white spot where they were attached to their bolster, to fall to the ground. Unlike the seeds of the sweet chestnut, those of the horse chestnut are inedible, even mildly poisonous when raw.

The leaves of the horse chestnut fall at the same time as the seeds: within a couple of days the trees may have lost all their foliage.

Taittinger was still looking at the golden chestnut leaf that had spiralled down onto the brim of Frau Matzner's purple hat. Not that he harbored any poetical inclinations. But on that moment he began to feel a strange, ridiculous affection for that wretched little leaf. It was a harbinger of autumn, clearly! How many times in his life had he seen such harbingers! But this one particular leaf was a harbinger to him, Taittinger, of his own personal autumn. He shuddered.

JOSEPH ROTH, *The Tale of the 1002nd Night*

The smaller North American variety *Aesculus glabra* grows abundantly in Ohio and is called *buckeye* there, because the brown nut peering through the half-open outer-shell resembles the winking eye of a deer.

The horse chestnut is grown mainly from seed, which germinates easily: in summer you can see many little saplings under chestnut trees or on compost heaps. If you want to grow a miniature chestnut forest in pots quickly, for planting out later in the garden or on the balcony, gather the conkers in the autumn and keep them in a tin of sand until the spring. This is to prevent them from sprouting or rotting. When digging them up in the spring, some will already have started to germinate. Soak them in water for a night (they will germinate even quicker then) and put them three at a time in a pot filled with soil.

If you wish to grow a mature tree, give it plenty of space in order to achieve its full majesty.

ETYMOLOGY

The origin of the name *horse* chestnut has given rise to much speculation (Clusius called it *Castanea equina*, *equina* meaning 'of the horse'); most convincing, however, is the suggestion that it derives from the horseshoe mark – complete with nail holes – left when each of last season's leaves fall. Another association with horses comes from the Middle and Near East (Turkey), where the tree is native and where short-windedness in horses was treated by feeding them horse chestnuts. In the United States vets still prescribe a remedy made of horse chestnuts for the treatment of the lungs and legs of horses.

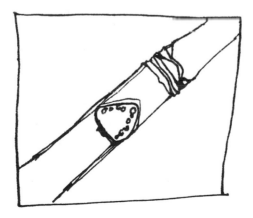

The mark on a horse-chestnut stem left by last year's leaf.

The word 'chestnut' is of course also used to indicate a certain type of horse and a hair colour – a dark reddish brown.

The water chestnut (*Eleocharis tuberosa*) has nothing to do with chestnuts, but is a bog plant of the sedge family much loved by the Chinese, cultivated for its edible root and available tinned in all Chinese grocery stores. Another water plant which is also eaten and also called water chestnut (to make it nicely confusing) is *Trapa natans*.

The jay his castanet has struck
Put on your muff for winter
The tippett that ignores his voice
Is impudent to nature
Of swarthy days he is the close
His lotus is a chestnut
The cricket drops a sable line
No more from yours at present

EMILY DICKINSON

USES

HOMEOPATHY AND OTHER ALTERNATIVE MEDICINE

The horse chestnut is cultivated for its bark and seeds, which are used in natural medicine. The ancient Greek physician and herbalist Dioscorides, whose *Materia Medica* dates from the 1st century AD, gave much space to the healing properties of horse chestnuts. Their beneficial effect when used in the form of a homeopathic ointment has been proved in the treatment of disorders of the circulation such as varicose veins and haemorrhoids. Research has also shown its benefits as an astringent and anti-inflammatory. It strengthens the capillary walls, thus reducing their permeability, and an extract of horse chestnut has been shown to improve the condition of connective tissue. An old American dispensary states that 'the action of buckeye (*Aesculus glabra*) is similar to, but more powerful than that of *Aesculus hippocastanum*, in its effects upon the portal circulation. It probably acts more powerfully on the spinal than upon the sympathetic nerves, it acts as a decided sedative.'

Horse chestnut also inhibits the development of oedema (swelling caused by accumulation of fluid in body tissue) and stimulates the circulatory system.

The *bark* of the horse chestnut tree can be applied to reduce fever or frostbite. The *seeds* have been employed successfully as an external remedy for rheumatism, as well as for painful cramps in the legs at night. In Japan, scientists have found that horse chestnuts have sufficient antioxidants to have potential as a treatment for wrinkles and, finally, in the United States a decoction of horse chestnut *leaves* is a traditional treatment for whooping cough.

Aesculina, a substance found in horse chestnut bark, protects the body against UV rays and is often used in suntan lotion.

The English alternative therapist Dr Edward Bach, who pioneered flower remedies, uses the white as well as the red horse chestnut flower. He reckons them to be most useful in the following circumstances:

> *For those who are unable to ban undesired thoughts, ideas from their minds [white].*
> *For those who don't learn from experience and keep making the same mistakes [the bud of the white].*
> *For those who suffer unwillingly for others,*

especially loved ones, and live in recurrent fear of a
car accident for example; for those who are always
fearing the worst [the red].

Cesar therapy is another field of alternative medicine that makes use of the horse chestnut. The seeds or nuts are dried for a month, then heated on a radiator or stove. The therapist puts the warm chestnuts in a cotton bag which he places it under the reclining patient's sacrum. Because it feels uncomfortable, the patient tries to relax as well as he or she can and by so doing cures himself of a lower backache. (Self-treatment is the essence of Cesar therapy.)

Some native Americans used to make a kind of snuff from horse chestnuts to relieve a cold; and they carried them as a protection against rheumatism and gout. This same remedy was once popular in Northern Europe – though in England it was deemed efficacious only if the chestnuts had been begged or stolen.

Another use of the *A. glabra* recorded in North America took advantage of its slight toxicity to stun fish in the water, in order to catch them more easily.

OTHER USES

Horse chestnuts have a high tannin content and have to be peeled and soaked in cold water for a night before use. Then they are drained and cooked for half an hour. Because they also contain saponin and colouring agents, they are frequently used in shampoo, to lend colour and shine to the hair.

Saponin is a cleansing agent, making chestnuts suitable as a detergent. People took advantage of this during World War II when there was no soap available in the shops. Housewives ground or grated the raw horse chestnuts and used the powder in their weekly wash, often with better results than the commercial stuff. It was noticed that the natural product was also effective against nappy rash.

Although the wood of the horse chestnut isn't suitable for burning and is of little economic value, in earlier times artificial limbs were often made from it, because it is light and easy to shape.

Adding a little ground horse chestnut to the can when watering house-plants keeps unwanted insects away from your pots.

> **NB** BE PRUDENT WITH SELF-REMEDY AND LIMIT YOURSELF TO EXTERNAL USE ONLY!

RECIPES FOR THE HOME DISPENSARY

HAIR CONDITIONER

>*100 g dried horse chestnut leaves*
>*1 litre water*

Boil the dried leaves for 5 minutes, then let them steep for 15 minutes. Strain the water and leave it to cool.

Apply to the hair after washing to give it a coppery shine. It also reduces dandruff.

A BATH TO RELIEVE RHEUMATISM

Gather plenty of horse chestnuts in the autumn, peel them, chop them finely and boil them for half an hour in plenty of water.

Strain through a coarse sieve and add this milky white fluid to a warm bath to relieve rheumatic pains.

CHILDREN'S TOYS

Chestnuts often feature in children's literature as the shiny brown seeds have a natural attraction. Chestnuts can be used to make little dolls and pipes and of course in the game called conkers.

To play conkers you need to bore a hole in a nicely symmetrical, fresh, hard horse chestnut. Pull a string through it and tie a knot in the end so it cannot slip out again. It is a game for two players. In turn, one player holds his conker still, at arm's length, while the other swings his own conker vigorously at the opponent's: the intention being to hit it. The game goes on until one of the conkers falls to bits.

He pulled from his pocket a black old horse chestnut hanging on a string. This old cobbler had 'cobbled' – hit and smashed – seventeen other cobblers on similar strings. So the boy was proud of his veteran.

D.H. LAWRENCE, *Sons and Lovers*

A now-celebrated horse chestnut is 'Anne Frank's tree' in the back garden of 263 Prinsengracht, Amsterdam. This is studiously maintained by the city authorities for its value as a tourist attraction. Apparently the Japanese, who have a strong tradition of tree-worship, try to get hold of a seed to take back home and grow an 'Anne Frank' sapling. From her hiding-place in the 'Achterhuis', the young diarist marked the passing seasons by watching this tree, which had been planted in 1845.

The horse chestnut 'candle' in full bloom.

II The sweet (or Spanish) chestnut, Castanea sativa

Châtaignier, marronnier – French
Castagno comune – Italian
Castaño – Spanish
Edel- oder Ess-Kastanie – German
Kasztan jadalny – Polish

For a character sketch of the sweet chestnut, I must first hand over to an earlier writer:

In the valley of the Tarn

A thin fringe of ash trees ran about the hill tops, like ivy on a ruin; but on the lower slopes, and far up every glen, the Spanish chestnut-trees stood each four-square to heaven under its tented foliage. Some were planted, each on its own terrace no larger than a bed; some, trusting in their roots, found strength to grow and prosper and be straight and large upon the rapid slopes of the valley; others, where there was a margin to the river, stood marshalled in a line and mightily like cedars of Lebanon. Yet even where they grew most thickly they were not to be thought of as a wood, but as a herd of stalwart individuals; and the dome of each tree stood forth separate and large, and as it were a little hill, from among the domes of its companions. They gave forth a faint sweet perfume which pervaded the air of the afternoon; autumn had put tints of gold and tarnish in the green; and the sun so shone through and kindled the broad foliage that each chestnut was relieved against another, not in shadow, but in light. A humble sketcher here laid down his pencil in despair.

I wish I could convey a notion of the growth of these noble trees; of how they strike out boughs like the oak, and trail sprays of drooping foliage like the willow; of how they stand on upright fluted columns like the pillars of a church; or like the olive, from the most shattered bole can put out smooth and youthful shoots, and begin a new life upon the ruins of the old. Thus they partake of the nature of many different trees; and even their prickly top-knots, seen near at hand against the sky, have a certain palm-like air that impresses the imagination. But their individuality, although compounded of so many elements, is but the richer and the more original. And to look down upon a level filled with these knolls of foliage, or to

*see a clan of old unconquerable chestnuts cluster 'like
herded elephants' upon the spur of a mountain, is
to rise to higher thoughts of the powers that are in
Nature.*

ROBERT LOUIS STEVENSON, *Travels with a Donkey*

This was written in September 1879, upon Stevenson's arrival in the Tarn valley – but travelling in
the Cévennes or the Ardèche regions of France
today you will be able to observe much the same
landscape, and in the autumn and winter many
roads are literally paved with chestnuts and their
hedgehog-like husks.

The Latin name of this tree, *Castanea*, was most
likely for the city of Kastanoea in Pontus in Asia
Minor (now Turkey), on the coast of the Black Sea.
The addition *sativa* means cultivated, 'that which
is sown or planted', and is attached to many food
plants, like *Oryza sativa* (rice) and *Lactuca sativa*
(lettuce).

GROWTH AND HABITAT

The sweet chestnut tree is a native of southern Europe, the Caucasus, Asia Minor and northern Africa. The young branches are reddish brown with light lenticels (pores in the bark), the leaves are elongated, feather-shaped and serrated, dark green on top and a lighter green underneath. The seeds – sweet chestnuts – grow in a green-brown cupule or outer shell with long spiky hairs which can be up to 5 centimetres long. Depending on the variety, one cupule may contain one to three seeds, which become brown when ripe, in October or November. The bark of the tree takes on a grey hue with age and is grooved and typically twisted. The sweet chestnut blooms in June or July, its blossom consisting of the male catkins, which are long, yellowish anthers, and the reddish female inflorescences. They appear in tufts long after all the leaves have come out, thus giving the trees the palmlike appearance mentioned by Stevenson. In order to bear fruit, the female flowers have to receive the pollen of another tree, carried by the wind, or by bees and other insects.

The sweet chestnut is a sister of the oak, and both belong to the beech family. A transitional form between the oak and the chestnut, *Quercus castaneifolia,* exists in Asia and the American northwest. Examples of this variety can be seen in Kew Gardens in London and in the Jardin des Plantes in Paris.

How fits his Umber Coat
The Tailor of the Nut?
Combined without a seam
Like Raiment of a Dream –

Who spun the Auburn Cloth?
Computed how the girth?
The Chestnut aged grows
In those primeval Clothes –

We know that we are wise
Accomplished in Surprise –
Yet by the Countryman –
This Nature – how undone!

EMILY DICKINSON

who described herself in a letter as follows:

My hair is bold like the chestnut burr, and my eyes
are like the sherry in the glass that the guest leaves.

CULTIVATION

The sweet chestnut – with the olive and the fig, the most characteristic tree of southern Europe – has always been of great economic importance, especially in Italy, France and Switzerland. It has been cultivated on a large scale for its nourishing fruit as well as for its wood. It is a 'sociable' tree, with a symbiotic relationship with many kinds of wild mushrooms; apart from chanterelles, boletus and russulas, one may also find chicken-of-the-woods, beefsteak fungus and the much-prized *Amanita caesaria* in a chestnut forest. In the south of France, chestnut groves in autumn are a favourite hunting-ground for wild boar, stuffing themselves with what the Greek philosopher Theophrastus called 'the acorn of Zeus'. In turn, these boar are hunted for the exquisite flavour the chestnuts add to their meat.

There are other species of sweet chestnut in other parts of the world. In America, there is the *C. dentata*; in China the *C. mollissima*; and in Japan the *C. crenata*. Of these, the Chinese produces the largest harvest of edible nuts, and the Japanese is the least palatable – however, its great advantage is resistance to chestnut blight. Scientists are engaged in the development of disease-resistant varieties of sweet chestnut trees, with higher yields. Because the sweet chestnut, apart from not liking frost, is not very choosy as far as soil is concerned and needs very little upkeep or control, it is a popular tree from an ecological viewpoint. It also serves as a protection against soil erosion.

I took refuge on the terraces, which are here greenly carpeted with sward, and tried to imitate with a pencil the inimitable attitudes of the chestnuts as they bear up their canopy of leaves. Ever and again a little wind went by, and the nuts dropped all around me, with a light and dull sound, upon the sward. The noise was as of a thin fall of great hailstones; but there went with it a cheerful human sentiment of an approaching harvest and farmers rejoicing in their gains. Looking up, I could see the brown nut peering through the husk, which was already gaping; and between the stems the eye embraced an amphitheatre of hill, sunlit and green with leaves.

ROBERT LOUIS STEVENSON

USES

The wood and the bark of the sweet chestnut contain a lot of tannin, which in Europe has been used for the colouring and tanning of hides. In the United States, where a chestnut blight caused by the fungus *Endothia parasitica* decimated chestnut woods at the beginning of the 20th century, a great effort has been made to cultivate a disease-resistant hybrid by crossing the native *C. dentata* with strains from China and Japan in order to replace the old woods, still standing as ghost forests. At about the same time, in southern Europe, plantations were thinned by tree canker combined with long periods of extreme frost. With the aim of checking further decrease, the first annual chestnut congress was organized in the French town of Brive-la-Gaillarde in 1924.

The tannin content of a mature sweet chestnut (a tree at least thirty years old) in southern Europe is 10 to 13 per cent higher than that of chestnut trees in the north. Italy has the largest commercial production of tannin.

The wood is very durable and serves, as the French say, literally *du berceau au cercueil*, 'from the cradle to the grave' (coffin). It is used for poles (for instance in the Kentish hop gardens), fence posts, railway sleepers, beams, garden furniture and, on account of being waterproof, for making wine barrels. Last but not least, let's not forget castanets, mostly cut from chestnut wood, as their name indicates.

> 'Tis likewise observed that this tree is so prevalent against cold, that where they stand, they defend other plantations from the injuries of the severest frosts: I am sure being planted in hedgerows etc., or for avenues to our country-houses, they are a magnificent and royal ornament.
>
> JOHN EVELYN, *Sylva* (1644)

HISTORY

The sweet chestnut – dedicated museums to which exist in Italy and France: the *Museo del Castagno* in Val di Roggio (Lucca) and the *Musée de la Châtaigneraie* in Joyeuse (Ardèche) – was native to Europe two million years ago. It became extinct in the Ice Age. Until relatively recently, it was commonly thought the ancient Romans had introduced the sweet chestnut to northern regions of Europe, until pollen dating back to the Iron Age (around the year 200 BC) was discovered. It is possible that the Celts, who at the time were already drinking wine from the south of France and trading back and forth across the Alps, knew the sweet chestnut and brought the seeds with them to grow in regions closer to home such as the Rhine, where wine was also made. In the Middle Ages, chestnut trees were cultivated by monasteries whose monks were busy raising herbs and other nutritious plants.

The natural speed of propagation of the sweet chestnut is an advance of from 2 to 3 kilometres per 100 years. Because the seed is so heavy it cannot be spread by animals or birds, therefore the chestnut landscape is entirely the work of mankind, and has often developed in parallel with viticulture.

Proof of the tree's early dietary importance, archaeologists tell us that the sweet chestnut was an important part of the daily fare of Roman legions, encamped in Noviomagus (the Dutch town of Nijmegen). Even today, many trees continue to thrive in the district, even if the rigours of a northern climate mean that not every year is blessed with an edible crop.

The Tree of the Hundred Horses

A METHUSELAH AMONG CHESTNUTS

In Southern France there's an old saying that goes:

One plants
a peach tree for oneself
an olive tree for one's son
a chestnut tree for one's grandson.

The oldest chestnut tree, one of the oldest trees in the world, grows on the island of Sicily, at an altitude of 550 metres on the eastern slope of the volcano Etna, in the vicinity of Sant'Alfio, and is known locally as *Il Castagno dei 100 Cavalli*, 'the tree of the hundred horses'. The legend has it that during a thunder storm, the queen of Aragon (or the queen of Anjou – there is some uncertainty which, since both royal houses once ruled Sicily) found shelter within its cavity for herself and the 100 horsemen who accompanied her on a visit to Mount Etna. This magnificent tree, which is estimated between 2000 and 4000 years-old, has been described since the 16th century in the diaries of many travellers, and sketched or painted by many artists. When the Scottish traveller Patrick Brydone, who was initially doubtful whether it was indeed a single tree, measured its girth in 1770, he found it to be 62 metres. The tree has withstood much abuse: from nature when showered with debris from Mount Etna, as well as from humans, presumably chestnut pickers, who built fires in its capacious and welcoming bole, and even built shacks or cabins in which to take shelter.

While I am writing this in chestnut country, the

Ardèche in France, I am surrounded by trees 'only' several hundred years old and I'm able to observe closely how they grow: the main trunk, often very thick and twisted, in many cases has died off, but the trees regenerate themselves by new shoots from the bottom, resulting in some cases in natural 'tree dwellings', cavities such as housed the pickers of Etna. What may appear to be a chestnut grove, in fact is often just one tree.

A Stone Age fossil of the chestnut variety *Castanea ungeri* found at Atanikerdluk in Greenland makes the Iron Age pollen mentioned earlier seem positively youthful. This can be seen in the Paleontological Museum in Oslo.

FOOD VALUE

> *But we give that fruit to our swine in England,*
> *which is amongst the delicacies of princes in other*
> *countries; the best tables in France and Italy make*
> *them a service, eating them with salt, in wine or juice*
> *of lemmon and sugar; being first roasted in embers*
> *on the chaplet; and doubtless we might propagate*
> *their use amongst our common people, being a food*
> *so cheap, and so lasting.*

JOHN EVELYN, *Sylva* (1644)

In certain regions of France the sweet chestnut used to be called *l'arbre à pain*, because people baked bread with the flour made by grinding chestnuts. Another name was *l'arbre à viande*, because pigs were fattened on them. Because of its nutritive value, this tree has played a significant rôle in the history of mankind since ancient times, doubtless helped by the fact that the seeds keep for quite a long time, without refrigeration or other care. Ancient physicians like Dioscorides and Galen and writers like Homer and Pliny the Elder described and prescribed it. In Germany also, where sweet chestnut trees grow especially abundantly in the Heidelberg region, chestnuts have been the *Kartoffel der Armen*, the poor man's potato. Goethe is known to have been extremely fond of chestnuts, which his mother sent to him every year by post, a tradition which, after her death, was continued by his son's landlady in Heidelberg.

> *Let us be many-sided! Turnips are good, but they are best together with chestnuts. And these two noble products of the earth grow far apart.*
>
> GOETHE

Sweet chestnuts are high in carbohydrates and they are the only nut to contain a significant amount of vitamin C (when uncooked, the same amount as lemon). For this reason it used to be a staple food against scurvy on long sea voyages.

MEDICINAL VALUE

The sweet chestnut, just as we have noticed with the horse chestnut, has medicinal value. It can be used as an antidote against the bite of a rabid dog, as well as against dysentery, coughing and vomiting, and baldness. It is also said to stimulate milk production in nursing mothers. Up to the 16th century is was recommended as an aphrodisiac in Arabic medicine.

A remedy for burns, allegedly originating from the crusaders who were in the habit of pouring boiling tar on their enemies, was to soften the leaves in hot water and, after cooling them in the open air, to apply them to the wound, which was then covered by swathes, kept moist and cool with tea. The tea detail must have been added later, because tea was not introduced into Europe until the 17th century. Perhaps in this case 'tea' meant an infusion of herbs or *tisane*.

In a Swedish herbal the sweet chestnut is also mentioned as a remedy for whooping cough. This book goes on to advise against its use by people with gall or liver problems or, indeed, a weak stomach.

PICKING AND DRYING CHESTNUT LEAVES

Select a tree in the spring, before it blooms, when the leaves are still fresh and soft. Wipe them clean if necessary (do not wash) and put them to dry on foil on a radiator or in another dry place like an attic or airing closet. Crumble the leaves, store them in little bottles or jars and keep them in a dark place. To apply make an infusion by boiling several teaspoons in water; strain them before use. Good to gargle with when afflicted with a sore throat.

I concealed myself, for all the world like a hunted Camisard, behind my fortification of vast chestnut trunk. I saw that I must be early awake; for these chestnut gardens had been the scene of industry no further gone than on the day before. The slope was strewn with lopped branches, and here and there a great package of leaves was propped against a trunk; for even the leaves are serviceable, and the peasants use them in winter by way of fodder for their animals.

ROBERT LOUIS STEVENSON, *Travels with a Donkey*

THE SWEET CHESTNUT
Nutritional value per 100 g

calories 191 – 307 (depending on the variety)
carbohydrates 41 5 g
fats 1.5 g
protein 2.8 g

Rich in starch, calcium, magnesium, potassium, phosphorus, iron, fibres and vitamins C, B1, B2 and E.

HARVESTING

Sweet chestnuts aren't picked, because they are ripe when they have fallen from the tree. To prevent infestation or other damage (chestnuts are half water), they shouldn't be left lying on the ground for a long time, especially in wet weather. Because it is a seed, the chestnut will want to germinate sooner or later, to ensure the survival of its kind. Where they are dealing with a large harvest, people put plastic sheet or netting beneath the trees to make gathering less burdensome.

When gathering or buying the nuts, look for nice hard shiny ones, which aren't dented or cracked.

They have to have a certain weight – if they're light and soft, or if they rattle, they have been kept for too long (in some cases since Christmas of the previous year).

STORAGE

Fresh sweet chestnuts can be kept for days in a cool place, and for weeks in the vegetable drawer of the refrigerator. They also keep well in a bowl of water for three weeks; refresh the water every other day. If they are kept like this a chemical reaction takes place which renders them more resistant to contamination. Animals bury them under a layer of leaves and we can follow their example – or lay them in a box filled with sand.

They can also be deep-frozen. To freeze them unpeeled, make an incision in each chestnut and first freeze them loose on a tray before bagging them up. They may be thrown in boiling water unthawed and then prepared for further use. You can also freeze them after you have peeled them.

PEELING

Carve a cross in each nut on the flat side, then boil them for 10 to 15 minutes in water with a little salt. Pour cold water over them the loosen both layers of skin and peel them with a tea towel as protection for your hands – chestnut skins can be very sharp. You can then purée them or freeze them whole.

An alternative is to roast the incised chestnuts on a tray in the oven at 200° C for about 20 to 30 minutes. Peel and/or freeze them as above.

If you are going to use them in recipes that don't call for whole chestnuts, you don't need to peel them in the prescribed manner. Instead, cut them in half with a sharp knife and cook them in boiling water as before. Scoop out the flesh with a spoon into a bowl of ice water – this facilitates the removal of the second, brown (and rather bitter) skin.

CHESTNUT FLOUR AND DRIED CHESTNUTS

In order to make flour from chestnuts they need to be dried and peeled first, an almost impossible job without the tools that have been invented for the purpose.

In France and Italy chestnuts were dried in special huts, called *clèdes* or *seccatoios*, on racks above a fire which was kept going for weeks, a method dating from at least the 14th century. In this way between one and ten tons of nuts could be dried at the same time, in layers 30 to 80 centimetres thick, turned over from time to time. After drying, the chestnuts were peeled and sorted according to size.

After the invention of the *décortiqueuse* or peeling machine in the 1920s, the chestnut industry ceased to be quite such hard labour.

Apart from chestnuts, *clèdes* were also used for drying wild mushrooms such as *cèpes*, and for storing apples. These days, drying is done on a much smaller scale, most likely in electric, gas- or oil-fired kilns. Many of the picturesque drying-huts have been converted to *gîtes*, where tourists or hikers can spend the night.

For making your own coarse meal at home, dried chestnuts are available in delicatessens and Chinese supermarkets. They can be crushed with a hammer first and then ground in a food processor. It is also possible to buy properly milled chestnut flour in many Italian shops.

If you are going to use dried chestnuts for any

other cookery, it is best to soak them overnight, and then boil them in the water used to soak them, as valuable vitamins will have leached into it.

Giacomo Castelvetro, whose 17th-century manuscript *The Fruit, Herbs and Vegetables of Italy* has been saved from oblivion by Gillian Riley, wrote:

> *We also cook chestnuts in good-quality sweet white wine, and when they are done strain them and put them to dry in the smoke. They are marvellous preserved this way, and last for a whole year.*

A clède, *or drying-house, for chestnuts.*

The monkey and the cat; engraving by GustaveDoré (1832–1883).

ROASTING CHESTNUTS

The monkey and the cat.

Sly Bertrand and Ratto in company sat,
(The one was a monkey, the other a cat,)
Co-servants and lodgers:
More mischievous codgers
Ne'er mess'd from a platter, since platters were flat.
Was anything wrong in the house or about it,
The neighbours were blameless, – no mortal could
doubt it;
For Bertrand was thievish, and Ratto so nice,
More attentive to cheese than he was to the mice.
One day the two plunderers sat by the fire,
Where chestnuts were roasting, with looks of
desire.
To steal them would be a right noble affair.
A double inducement our heroes drew there--
'Twould benefit them, could they swallow their fill,
And then 'twould occasion to somebody ill.
Said Bertrand to Ratto, 'My brother, to-day
Exhibit your powers in a masterly way,
And take me these chestnuts, I pray.
Which were I but otherwise fitted

(As I am ingeniously witted)
For pulling things out of the flame,
Would stand but a pitiful game.'
''Tis done,' replied Ratto, all prompt to obey;
And thrust out his paw in a delicate way.
   First giving the ashes a scratch,
   He open'd the coveted batch;
Then lightly and quickly impinging,
He drew out, in spite of the singeing,
One after another, the chestnuts at last,—
While Bertrand contrived to devour them as fast.
A servant girl enters. Adieu to the fun.
Our Ratto was hardly contented, says one.—

No more are the princes, by flattery paid
For furnishing help in a different trade,
   And burning their fingers to bring
   More power to some mightier king.

JEAN DE LA FONTAINE, *Fables*

This is the source of the saying 'pulling someone's chestnuts out of the fire'.

According to an old Anglo-Saxon custom, young girls would carve the initials of admired young men on chestnuts, which they put in the fire,

Maidens, name your chestnuts true.
The first to burst belongs to you!

Chestnuts, bursting with love: what could be a better symbol for the simplest way to cook them? Simple it may be, but roasting chestnuts is more than just throwing them into the fire: even the most elementary methods need attention, if only in the selection of the ingredient.

In the chestnut regions of France and Italy people use a special chestnut pan for roasting them: it is cast iron, with a long handle and holes – slightly smaller than a chestnut – in the bottom.

The roasting time depends on the variety and size of the chestnuts, the intensity of the heat and the distance between chestnut and fire. It can be anything from 15 to 30 minutes. Turn them regularly or keep shaking the pan.

Someone thought of a cunning trick to tell when chestnuts are done. They explode if they aren't nicked first, so leaving one of the nuts uncut will signal when they are done. Note well, however, if you use this method, be sure to keep some distance from the fire: the explosion can be quite loud and provoke a rain of sharp shells!

PETRUCHIO:
And you tell me of a woman's tongue
That gives not half so great a blow to hear
As will a chestnut in a farmer's fire?

SHAKESPEARE, *The Taming of the Shrew*

A chestnut roasting pan.

Many will think fondly of chestnut vendors in the streets of London; and whoever wanders round Paris in the autumn will have a hard time resisting the alluring scent of roasting chestnuts pervading squares and boulevards.

Of all nuts the sweet chestnut is the best protected: it is hidden in three layers of armour – a bitter brown skin, a hard shell that can tear your hands, and an outer husk with hairs as prickly as a hedgehog. Roasting chestnuts, gathered round the hearth, is a good way of dodging the chore of preparation, for everyone pulls their own nuts from the fire and peels them in a tea towel or napkin while the next portion is roasting. In the south of France it is the custom to ask the youngest in the company to sit on a parcel of freshly roasted chestnuts wrapped in a towel. This loosens the skins. With a glass of young wine – chestnuts ripen at the same season as the Beaujolais *primeur* is uncorked – some pâté, cheese and fruit, chestnuts make for one of the most delicious, nutritious and sociable meals.

The only other outstanding memory I have of my time at Wiveliscombe Primary School was when, in the milk break one autumn day, I placed a dozen shiny brown chestnuts on the potbellied stove in the corner of the classroom. I had spent the previous Sunday knocking them out of the trees by the reservoir with a stick with the intention of roasting them and eating them before class started again. Unfortunately I forgot, and halfway through a writing exercise, where only the scratching of nibs on paper disturbed the heavy silence, the chestnuts suddenly exploded like a burst of machine-gun fire. The teacher was panic-stricken. After she regained her composure and restored order after the pandemonium that my intended snack had caused, I, of course, spent the rest of the lesson with my hands on my head, standing in the corner. She was, of course, convinced that I had done it deliberately.

KEITH FLOYD, *Out of the Frying Pan. An Autobiography*

CHÂTAIGNE OR *MARRON?*

In French and Italian there are two different names for edible chestnuts, to distinguish (morphologically as well as biologically) between two kinds: *châtaigne* and *marron* (French) and *castagno* and *marrone* (Italian). The European sweet chestnut is a fruitful strain with more than seven hundred varieties, the most important difference being that the *marron* or *marrone* is the bigger and fatter cousin, primarily used to make the well-known *marrons glacés*. In Italy, which has 800,000 hectares of chestnut wood, sugared chestnuts are called *marrone Piemonte*. The *marron* is a variety carefully cultivated for its size, ease of peeling and texture. Among specialists there is an ongoing debate whether the *marron* is actually fuller and sweeter than the *châtaigne*, but as *marrons* are usually coated with a thick layer of sugar, this seems of minor importance.

More importantly, the *marron* grows as a single nut in one outer shell, whereas a regular chestnut cupule may contain up to three seeds, each in a separate compartment, flatter than marrons. Usually, one of these triplets has appropriated all the nutritional value, leaving the others as no more than flat, empty skins.

Recently the Ardèche chestnut has obtained an *Appellation d'Origine Contrôlée* so ensuring its quality and provenance is protected under French (and EU) law in much the same manner as French wines have been since the 1930s.

Apart from *marrons glacés*, fat chestnuts are used to make *purée de marron* or *crème de marron*, available in those beautiful ribbed tins from the house of Clément Faugier, established in Privas in 1882.

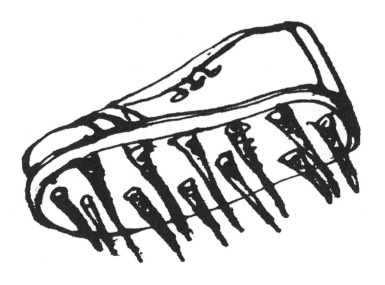

'Las solas', *shoes designed for peeling chestnuts* en masse.

When the chestnuts were ripe I laid up half a bushel for winter. It was very exciting at that season to roam the then boundless chestnut woods of Lincoln – they now sleep their long sleep under the railroad – with a bag on my shoulder, and a stick to open burrs with in my hand, for I did not always wait for the frost, amid the rustling of leaves and the loud reproofs of the red squirrels and the jays, whose half-consumed nuts I sometimes stole, for the burrs they had selected were sure to contain sound ones. Occasionally I climbed and shook the trees.

They grew also behind my house, and one large tree, which almost overshadowed it, was, when in flower, a bouquet which scented the whole neighborhood, but the squirrels and the jays got most of the fruit; the last coming in flocks early in the morning and picking the nuts out of the burrs before they fell.

HENRY DAVID THOREAU

A chestnut peeling machine.

III Recipes for sweet chestnuts

FIRST COURSES
Terrine of chestnuts and wild mushrooms
Curly endive with chestnuts
Chanterelle mushrooms with chestnuts
Savoury cake with bacon and olives

SOUP
Pumpkin-chestnut soup
Chestnut soup with Madeira
Russian chestnut soup with *quenelles*
Consommé Nesselrode

CHESTNUTS AND VEGETABLES
Chestnuts with Brussels sprouts
Hungarian chestnuts
Chestnuts with cabbage
Chestnuts with lentils, Roman-style
Chestnuts with potatoes
Chestnuts with sweet potatoes

STUFFINGS
Basic stuffing for poultry 1
Basic stuffing for poultry 2

Chestnut stuffing with apples and lemon
Chestnut stuffing with prunes and brandy
Chestnut stuffing with apricots and mushrooms
Turkish stuffing for shoulder of lamb

FISH, POULTRY AND MEAT
Autumn trout
Quail with chestnuts and calvados
Pasta with chestnut sauce
Lamb with chestnuts
Stuffed pancakes
Veal with chestnuts
Guinea fowl with chestnuts and cabbage

BREAD, CAKES AND DESSERTS WITH CHESTNUT FLOUR
Chestnut bread
Chestnut polenta
Castagnaccio
Apple-chestnut *clafoutis*
Chestnut cake with walnuts
Chestnut cookies

BREAD, CAKES AND DESSERTS WITH WHOLE CHESTNUTS
Chestnut bread
Basic recipe for *crème* and *purée de marron*

Mont Blanc
Monet's chestnut cookies
Drunken chestnuts
Chestnuts in Marsala
Chestnut tart
Chestnut-nutmeg tart
Marrons glacés

WEIGHTS AND MEASURES

The cups and spoons used in this book are equal to the following measures:

1 teaspoon = 5 ml
1 tablespoon = 15 ml (1.5 cl)
¼ cup = 60 ml (6 cl)
⅓ cup = 80 ml (8 cl)
½ cup = 120 ml (12 cl; 1.2 dl)
1 cup = 240 ml (24 cl; 24 dl)
2 cups = 480 ml (48 cl; 4.8 dl)
4 cups = 960 ml (96 cl; 9.6 dl)
1 coffee cup = 100 ml (10 cl)

Unless otherwise stated, the recipes are calculated to serve 4 people.

To avoid repeating the cooking and peeling instructions for fresh chestnuts in each recipe, I refer you to the earlier pages of this chapter.

Chestnuts are also available tinned – either in water or vacuum-packed – vacuum-packed in plastic, or dried. Those tinned in water tend to be soggy and lack flavour. Dried ones, although they have the disadvantage of having to soak overnight, come closest to the fresh nuts, in consistency as well as flavour.

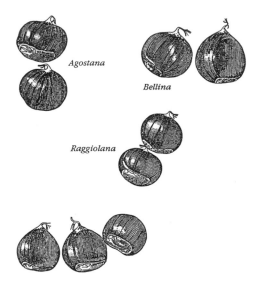

Agostana

Bellina

Raggiolana

FIRST COURSES

> *A sailor's wife had chestnuts in her lap*
> *And munch'd and munch'd and munch'd. -*

SHAKESPEARE, *Macbeth*

☙ TERRINE OF CHESTNUTS AND WILD MUSHROOMS

Depending on the weather and the region you live in, there may already be chestnuts available in the late autumn, when there are still plenty of different kinds of wild mushrooms to be found in the woods. You can use any sort of mushroom for this recipe, including ordinary cultivated ones bought from the shops – but in general, the wilder the better!

> *100 g mushrooms*
> *1 tablespoon oil*
> *1 onion, chopped*
> *salt, freshly ground black pepper*
> *300 g chestnuts, cooked and peeled*
> *25 g butter*
> *freshly grated nutmeg*
> *bay leaves, 5 or 6 juniper berries*

Clean the mushrooms by wiping them with a damp cloth; never rinse mushrooms, for they become soggy. Slice them.

Put a thin layer of oil in a frying-pan and glaze the onion over a medium heat. Add the sliced mushrooms and let them fry gently for about 15 minutes. Season with salt and pepper.

Purée the chestnuts in a food processor or *mouli-légumes*. If they seem too dry for the machinery to work satisfactorily, moisten them with a little of their cooking water.

Add the butter and the chestnut purée to the onions and mushrooms in the pan.

Stir in a little nutmeg and pack the mixture in an earthenware terrine. Decorate the top with bay leaves and juniper berries.

Leave the mixture to set in the refrigerator.

Serve at room temperature together with some pickled onions, gherkins and toasted (chestnut) bread.

❧ CURLY ENDIVE SALAD WITH CHESTNUTS

> *1 head of curly endive, also called* escarole *or* frisée
> *1 thick slice of smoked streaky bacon (about 50 g)*
> *1 tablespoon olive oil*
> *200 g chestnuts, cooked and peeled*
> *a vinaigrette dressing of olive oil, French mustard,*
> *tarragon vinegar, salt and pepper*

Wash and dry the greens and tear them up in a salad bowl.

Cut the bacon into strips or cubes and fry in the olive oil until crisp. Just before they are browned, add the chestnuts to give them a bit of colour.

Remove the bacon and chestnuts with a slotted spoon and arrange on top of the salad.

Make a vinaigrette dressing and serve it separately. (Undressed salad will keep for another day if left over.)

CHANTERELLE MUSHROOMS WITH CHESTNUTS

This seasonally well-matched pair makes a perfect side-dish with game. As the French say: 'Les girolles sont fidèles' – chanterelles are faithful – referring to the fact that they always come up in the same place, so once you've found such a spot, you can be reasonably sure of a yearly harvest.

90 g butter
500 g chanterelle mushrooms, brushed and sliced
18 chestnuts, cooked, peeled and sliced
¼ cup dry sherry
a few drops of Tabasco
salt, freshly ground pepper
fresh herbs such as parsley, chives or marjoram

Melt the butter in a frying-pan and fry the mushrooms until they have exuded their juice.

Add the chestnuts and fry for another 5 minutes.

Pour the sherry and the Tabasco into the pan and season everything with salt and pepper. Sizzle and toss to amalgamate all the ingredients.

Decorate with some freshly chopped herbs.

🐛 SAVOURY CAKE WITH BACON AND OLIVES

(for 6–8 people)

> *4 eggs*
> *150 g butter*
> *125 g flour*
> *125 g chestnut flour*
> *150 g stoned green olives*
> *150 g smoked bacon*
> *150 g Gruyère cheese, grated*
> *2 tablespoons dry white wine*
> *approx. 2 teaspoons baking powder*
> *pepper*

Separate the eggs. Beat the yolks with the butter until creamy.

Add both kinds of flour, the olives cut into rings, the bacon cut into strips, the grated cheese, the wine, the baking powder and a little black pepper. Mix thoroughly.

Beat the egg whites until stiff and fold them carefully into the batter.

Put the batter in a buttered cake tin and immediately put in a preheated oven. Bake for 20 minutes at 180° C, and then for another hour at 160° C.

SOUPS

From prickly foliage
You fell down
complete,
polished wood,
gleaming mahogany.

PABLO NERUDA

Because of their texture and richness chestnuts form a good base for a soup, from a simple bouillon with onion, garlic and a few herbs, to the fancy consommé Nesselrode, to which a whole history is attached, as you will see later.

PUMPKIN-CHESTNUT SOUP

A market woman selling vegetables in a town in the Ardèche gave me this recipe. This soup, which makes for a very tasty start to an autumn or winter meal, may be made with water or chicken stock. With the addition of a simple green salad and a slice of coarse *pain de campagne*, it will serve as a main dish.

30 g butter
1 onion, chopped
1 thin leek or half a thick one, cleaned and sliced
1 stalk celery, chopped
400 g pumpkin (weight without skin and seeds)
400 g peeled chestnuts
chicken stock or water
approx. 65 ml crème frâiche
salt, pepper, nutmeg, fresh sage leaves

Melt the butter in a large soup pan and glaze the chopped onion and leek until they have become transparent. Add the chopped celery and a little salt and let the vegetables fry gently on low heat for 5 minutes.

Cut the pumpkin into cubes and add to the pan with the chestnuts. Stir well and fry everything together for a few minutes.

Add enough water or stock to cover the vegetables, bring to a boil, turn down the heat and let simmer until the vegetables are tender (about 20 to 30 minutes).

Purée the soup in a food processor or with a *mouli-légumes*. Season, if necessary, with some extra salt, pepper and nutmeg and stir in the *crème frâiche* just before serving. The silvery green of a few fresh sage leaves contrasts attractively with the delicate orange of the soup.

For a special touch, pour in a drop of *Pastis* if you happen to have it.

❧ CHESTNUT SOUP WITH MADEIRA

The nutty-sweet taste of parsnips goes well with chestnuts and the Madeira.

120 g butter
2 leeks, cleaned and sliced
2 parsnips, peeled and chopped
4 cups chestnuts, cooked and peeled
salt, pepper, ground allspice
½ cup Madeira
6 cups chicken or veal stock
4 tablespoons single cream
flat-leaved parsley

Melt the butter in a soup pan and glaze the leeks for 5 minutes. Add the parsnips and chestnuts and season with salt, pepper and a pinch of allspice. Stir well and let everything fry gently for about 10 minutes.

First pour in the Madeira, then the stock. Bring to a boil, reduce the heat and let the soup simmer for a quarter hour or longer, until the chestnuts are tender.

Purée the soup and adjust the seasoning. Stir in the cream just before serving and garnish with some flat-leaved parsley.

RUSSIAN CHESTNUT SOUP WITH *QUENELLES*

Quenelles are poached meat or fish balls which are served sliced in a soup. It is advisable to make the quenelles first, before you start on the soup.

For the quenelles
250 g cooked beef, veal or chicken
butter for frying
½ onion, chopped
2 slices French bread
dash of milk
1 egg yolk
¼ teaspoon black pepper
½ teaspoon salt
pinch of nutmeg
1 tablespoon butter (or sour cream)

For the soup
500 g chestnuts
1 litre stock
2 egg yolks
½ cup single cream
salt, pepper
1 glass white wine
freshly chopped parsley or chives

For the *quenelles* mince the meat finely and fry it gently in the butter with the chopped onion.

Soak the bread in a dash of milk, squeeze it dry and add it to the meat together with the egg yolk.

Season with salt, pepper and a little nutmeg and mash the butter or sour cream into the dough. Purée the mixture in a food processor or rub it through a fine sieve.

Roll the dough in a piece of muslin or cheese cloth and shape it into a sausage. Tie it at both ends and poach it for about seven minutes in boiling water.

Leave to cool, remove the cloth and slice the sausage thinly into individual *quenelles*.

For the soup, nick and peel the chestnuts as previously described; pour stock over them until they're just covered and let them simmer for 15 minutes until very tender.

Rub them through a sieve, add the rest of the stock and stir well.

Beat the egg yolks into the cream and pour slowly into the soup while stirring. Season with salt and pepper. Ensure the soup doesn't boil after you have added the egg yolk liaison.

Just before serving, pour in the wine and add the sliced *quenelles*. Scatter with parsley or chives.

CONSOMMÉ NESSELRODE

As chancellor in St. Petersburg during the reign of Czar Alexander I in the first half of 19th century, Karl Robert Nesselrode, a Russian count of German origin, had great influence. This was a period when French culture reigned supreme, not only in the spheres of language and fashion, but also haute cuisine.

The Frenchman Jean Mouy, Nesselrode's personal chef, was considered one of the most inspired cooks of his time in Russia. It was he who invented the famously outrageous *Bombe Nesselrode*, one of the richest puddings ever (made with thirty-two eggs), which indeed may have the effect of an explosive device. According to legend, another famous cook, Carême, was so jealous of his colleague's recipe that they were continually at odds.

Here is his recipe for the classic soup, dedicated to his master.

480 ml chicken stock
30 g celery, chopped
250 g chestnuts, cooked and peeled
250 g onions, chopped
180 g butter

1 generous cup Béchamel sauce (recipe below)
salt, nutmeg, white pepper
60 ml single cream
50 g mushrooms, chopped
4 small bread rolls, halved and hollowed out
1000 ml of the finest beef or game consommé

Put the chicken stock with the celery in a saucepan, bring to a boil and add the chestnuts. Cook for 5 minutes until the chestnuts are very tender and drain. Reserve the broth for another dish and mash or purée the chestnuts.

In another pan, blanch the onions in boiling water for about 7 minutes. Drain well.

Melt two thirds of your butter in a frying-pan and sauté the onions in this until they begin to brown. Add the béchamel sauce and season with salt, pepper and nutmeg. Simmer for 5–6 minutes, stirring occasionally. Add the chestnuts and rub the entire mixture through a sieve with the aid of a wooden spoon.

Reheat this purée and add the chopped mushrooms, the remaining butter and cream. Blend well. (This mixture is known as an onion-chestnut *soubise*.)

Heat the hollow bread rolls in the oven and, shortly before the final service, fill them with the *soubise*.

Heat the consommé, ladle it out in separate soup plates and float two halves of each roll in every plate.

ぞ BÉCHAMEL SAUCE

Legend has it that this sauce was named for the financier Louis de Béchameil, marquis de Nointel and *maître d'hôtel* to Louis XIV.

50 g butter
50 g flour
250 ml hot milk
1 small carrot, quartered
1 small onion, quartered
2 cloves
1 bouquet garni (*a branch of thyme, parsley, marjoram, bay leaf*)
salt, black pepper

Melt the butter, stir in the flour and cook for 2 minutes on low heat while stirring constantly, without browning the mixture.

Carefully stir in one spoonful of milk, then a little more, and so on until all the milk is used up. Keep stirring.

Add the rest of the ingredients and cook for 15 minutes until the sauce has reached the desired consistency and flavour. Strain before use.

CHESTNUTS WITH VEGETABLES

> *And what I used to eat at mother's:*
> *Chestnuts, braised in cabbage!*
> *Deliciously swimming in butter,*
> *Locally dried cod: be praised!*

HEINRICH HEINE

CHESTNUTS WITH BRUSSELS SPROUTS

A classic combination, a must with the Christmas bird; this version has a Canadian touch.

> *3 cups small white pickling onions or shallots, peeled*
> *3 cups small sprouts*
> *½ cup maple syrup*
> *2 tablespoons tarragon vinegar*
> *3 cups chestnuts, peeled and cooked*
> *½ teaspoon freshly ground black pepper*

With a small knife, make a cross in the root ends of the onions and sprouts.

Bring water to the boil in a pan and blanch the onions for about 4 minutes. Remove them with a slotted spoon and put them in a bowl. Blanch the sprouts in the same water for 4 minutes. Strain into a colander and rinse with cold water (to preserve their fresh green colour).

Heat the maple syrup in a saucepan, add the onions and the vinegar. Lower the heat and let the onions simmer for about 20 minutes, until the liquid has almost evaporated.

Add the chestnuts and sprouts to the onions. Mix well and simmer them for about 5 more minutes until all the vegetables are heated through. Don't overcook! Season with salt and pepper.

❧ HUNGARIAN CHESTNUTS

> *25 g butter*
> *1 onion, chopped*
> *250 g chestnuts, cooked and peeled*
> *2 large sweet red peppers, cut into strips*
> *250 g fresh mushrooms*
>   *or 25 g dried cèpes/porcini mushrooms*
> *100 ml stock*
> *salt, pepper*
> *4 tablespoons sour cream*
> *fresh herbs such as chives, parsley or marjoram*

Melt the butter in a frying-pan and fry the onion until transparent. Add the chestnuts and red pepper and let everything fry gently for 2–3 minutes on a low heat.

Add the mushrooms and the stock. (Dried mushrooms have to be reconstituted in a bowl of hot water for 10-15 minutes first.) Cover and let simmer for 20 minutes.

Season to taste and stir in the sour cream just before serving. Sprinkle with some chopped fresh herbs.

CHESTNUTS WITH CABBAGE

An Auvergnat dish which goes under the dialect-name *Castanhas riuladas*. Simple but heartwarming winter food, with two well-matched ingredients.

> *1 head of cabbage, the curly kind (Savoy)*
> *1 kg chestnuts, peeled*
> *salt*

Remove the outer leaves of the cabbage and rinse them well. Line the bottom and sides of a large pan with them.

Add the chestnuts to the pan and cover them with the rest of the cabbage leaves. Season with salt. Add sufficient water so the pan does not boil dry, put the lid on the pan and let the chestnuts stew on a very low heat for three quarters of an hour.

CHESTNUTS WITH LENTILS, ROMAN-STYLE

Pliny the Elder wrote: 'I find the authorities on the subject consider that the eating of lentils promotes an even temper.'

This is a recipe from *Apicius*, the only significant recipe text that has survived from the days of the Roman empire, compiled in the late 4th or early 5th century AD. It is a variation on his dish *Lenticulam de castaneis*. Quite a few translated and adapted versions of *Apicius* have been published and, for those interested in the history of food and cooking, he offers an unmatched wealth of detailed information, especially in the sphere of herbs and wild plants and roots.

As was often the case in antiquity, the herbs people used had medicinal as well as culinary value. Pennyroyal is a kind of mint which was used to bring round people who had fainted and as a stimulant in the event of fatigue; it would be hung in bunches in the house or taken as a precaution on long journeys. Like pennyroyal, rue, once considered one of the most valuable medicinal herbs, has also fallen into disuse. In Italy, it is still used sometimes to flavour grappa.

200 g brown lentils
600 ml beef or vegetable stock
200 g peeled chestnuts
½ teaspoon ground pepper
¼ teaspoon cumin seed
½ teaspoon coriander seed
1 ½ teaspoons mint

½ teaspoon each of rue (or rosemary, if you don't happen to have rue in the garden), pennyroyal and fennel
1 teaspoon wine vinegar
1 tablespoon honey
2 tablespoon olive oil

Cook the lentils in the stock until tender. Drain and save the stock.

Take another pan and just cover the chestnuts with cold water. Bring to a boil and simmer until tender. Drain the chestnuts and slice them.

Using a pestle and mortar, grind the pepper, cumin, coriander, mint, rue (or rosemary), fennel (and pennyroyal if available). Moisten with the vinegar and blend in the honey.

Put the chestnuts and the lentils with the herb sauce in a pan and add 120 ml of the stock you have reserved. Simmer for 5 minutes.

Season to taste with more vinegar or more honey, and stir in the olive oil just before serving.

CHESTNUTS WITH POTATOES (*GRATIN AUVERGNAT*)

This upgraded version of mash is good company to roast fowl, meat, or sausages. It is originally made with Cantal cheese from the mountains of Auvergne, but Gruyère is a good substitute.

> *500 g potatoes*
> *172–250 ml milk*
> *500 g chestnuts, peeled and cooked*
> *30 g butter*
> *salt, freshly ground black pepper*
> *100 g grated Cantal or Gruyère cheese*

Peel the potatoes and boil them until soft. Mash them with about 100 ml milk.

Mash the chestnuts with about 75 ml milk till they have about the same consistency as the potatoes.

Mix the two mashes, add the butter and season with salt and pepper. Mix thoroughly.

Butter an oven dish and put in the mash. Sprinkle with grated cheese; the top has to be well covered. Dot with cubes of butter and heat in a medium hot oven (190° C) until nicely brown on top.

CHESTNUTS WITH SWEET POTATOES

In Japan, a friend tells me, it is a tradition on New Year's Eve to make *Kuri-Kinton*, a purée of steamed sweet potatoes with coarsely chopped chestnuts. It is then coloured a bright yellow with gardenia seeds. Each guest receives his portion in one of those gorgeous lacquer bowls.

The following mash is very tasty with game or roast fowl.

500 g sweet potatoes
50 g butter
200 ml milk
500 g chestnuts, cooked, peeled and mashed
1 egg
dash of dry sherry
salt, white pepper, cayenne pepper

Peel the potatoes and boil them until tender. Mash them together with the butter and the warmed milk.

Beat the mashed chestnuts with the mashed potatoes, add the egg and the sherry and season with salt, pepper and a pinch of cayenne pepper.

STUFFINGS

> *While hisses on my hearth the pulpy pear,*
> *And black'ning chestnuts start and crackle there.*

JOHN MILTON

STUFFINGS FOR FOWL

Stuffings can elevate poultry – from a little quail to a turkey – to the level of a very aromatic and festive dish by means of a variety of fruit, herbs, spices and mushrooms. You can experiment to your heart's content, but to help you along I will give two basic recipes with which to start.

è❧ BASIC STUFFING I

This makes enough to stuff a chicken, guinea-fowl or a small turkey of 4–5 kilograms. You can add herbs or garlic to taste.

> *500 g chestnuts, cooked and peeled*
> *2 onions, chopped*
> *2 tablespoons fresh sage, or 1 teaspoon dried*
> *100 g soft breadcrumbs*
> *salt, pepper*

100 g streaky smoked bacon, without rind
400 g pork sausage meat or sausages without their
  skins
150 ml brandy

Chop the chestnuts coarsely

Mix the chestnuts with the onions, sage and breadcrumbs; season with salt and pepper.

Cut the bacon in cubes or strips and remove the meat from the sausage skins. Knead this mixture with the chestnuts and onions.

Stir in the brandy

The bird which is to be improved by this stuffing has to roast for at least 1 hour so that the sausage meat is completely cooked – unless you are merely putting a few teaspoons into a quail, for example.

If you have any of the stuffing mixture left over after you have filled the bird's cavity, it can be deep-frozen in readiness for the next occasion.

BASIC STUFFING 2

This is a meatless version, to which you can add other ingredients of your choice to make a more luxurious affair.

> *butter, olive oil*
> *2 onions, chopped*
> *3 ribs of celery, sliced and diced*
> *2 medium-sized carrots, sliced and diced*
> *1 parsnip, peeled and finely diced*
> *thyme, bay leaf, salt, pepper*
> *half a stale loaf of French bread, cut into cubes*
> *500 g chestnuts, cooked, peeled and chopped*

Heat half butter, half olive oil in a deep pan with a heavy bottom. Soften the onion and add the celery, carrot, parsnip and herbs. Let simmer gently for about 15 minutes and season with salt and pepper.

Stir in the coarsely chopped chestnuts and the cubed bread and moisten with a little extra olive oil.

Leave the mixture to cool before stuffing the bird.

CHESTNUT STUFFING WITH APPLES AND LEMON

Start with the ingredients list of the first basic stuffing recipe above, then add the following:

4 large cloves of garlic
2 apples, chopped
5 tablespoons freshly chopped parsley
1 teaspoon fresh thyme, leaves picked off the stalks
grated rind and juice of 1 lemon
1-2 eggs, beaten

Combine all these with the basic stuffing mixture and use with a bird of your choice. An orange may be substituted for the lemon.

CHESTNUT STUFFING WITH PRUNES AND BRANDY

This is exquisite with guinea-fowl.

To either of the basic stuffing recipes I have given above, you simply add 100 g dried prunes, first soaked in brandy.

🐦 CHESTNUT STUFFING WITH APRICOTS AND CHESTNUT MUSHROOMS

What are known as chestnut mushrooms are sometimes called brown caps in British supermarkets. They are cultivated mushrooms, but have a stronger taste and deeper colour than the usual button mushroom.

> *2 tablespoons olive oil*
> *1 large onion, chopped*
> *2 ribs of celery, chopped*
> *100 g chestnut mushrooms (wiped clean with a*
>   *moist towel, then sliced)*
> *2 teaspoons rosemary, chopped*
> *200 g chestnuts, cooked, peeled and chopped*
> *100 g dried apricots, chopped*
> *1 egg, beaten*
> *50 g breadcrumbs*

Heat the oil and fry the onion and celery for about 7 minutes until soft. Stir in the mushrooms and rosemary and fry gently until the mushrooms are done.

Add the chestnuts and apricots and stir well.

Take the pan from the heat and stir in the egg and

breadcrumbs. Season with salt and pepper.

Leave to cool before stuffing a turkey or other bird.

If you have a little of the mixture left over, you can roll it into little balls which you can roast around the bird in the pan.

❧ TURKISH STUFFING FOR SHOULDER OF LAMB

My Turkish butcher gave me this recipe; he claims the shoulder and the shank are the juiciest and most tender parts of the lamb. Have your butcher make a pocket in a shoulder of lamb, by separating the meat from the blade at one end. The quantities given are calculated for a reasonably large piece of meat, but if you have any stuffing left over, you can freeze it and use it for poultry or other joints.

> *10 chestnuts, cooked and peeled*
> *½ cup shelled pistachio nuts*
> *1 cup of cooked rice*
> *½ cup currants*
> *salt, pepper, cayenne pepper*
> *½ teaspoon cinnamon*
> *butter*

Chop the chestnuts and pistachios and mix them with the other ingredients.

Melt the butter and fry the stuffing very gently on low heat.

Fill the pocket of the shoulder with the stuffing and if necessary fasten with toothpicks.

A barrel, illustrated in Diderot's Encyclopédie, *such as was used by French spur-makers in the 18th century to wash their metalwork. Chestnut was a popular choice for barrel-staves as the wood was tough and water-resistant. Hence, too, its use on farms for fence posts as it would last much longer in the ground than other timbers.*

FISH, POULTRY AND MEAT

AUTUMN TROUT

A rare combination of chestnuts and fish, which could be tried with other kinds of freshwater fish as well as some of the tropical varieties – tilapia, Victoria bass, red snapper – that are available in the markets.

> *300 g chestnuts*
> *500 ml milk*
> *250 g fresh spinach*
> *60 g butter, and some cubes to finish*
> *300 g chanterelle mushrooms (optional)*
> *1 small piece of pork fat (about 50 g)*
> *2 shallots, chopped*
> *4 tablespoons* crème frâiche
> *salt, pepper*
> *1 trout per person*
> *juice of 1 lemon*

Scald and peel the chestnuts as previously described. Boil them a little longer in the milk.

In the meantime blanch the spinach and drain it in a colander.

Melt half the butter and fry the chanterelles, which you have wiped or brushed clean, together with the cubed pork fat and the shallots until all the liquid has evaporated.

Sprinkle the trout with lemon juice and fry in the rest of the butter until brown on both sides, but not completely done (about 2 minutes on each side).

Chop the chestnuts and the spinach and stir them through the chanterelles mixture. Finish by adding the *crème fraîche*. Put half of this mixture on the bottom of a buttered oven dish. Put the fish on top and cover with the rest of it.

Dot with cubes of butter and put the dish in a preheated oven (200° C). The fish will be done (depending on the size, of course) in approximately 10 minutes.

QUAIL WITH CHESTNUTS AND CALVADOS

The apples and Calvados betray the Norman origin of this dish.

> *8 quail*
> *salt and pepper*
> *2 apples, peeled, cored and diced*
> *1 onion, sliced*
> *1 bay leaf*
> *300 g chestnuts, cooked, peeled and chopped*
> *3 tablespoons Calvados*
> *chicken stock*
> *fresh marjoram, or other herbs*

Preheat the oven to 200° C. Season the quail with salt and pepper and stuff with the diced apple. Put them in a buttered oven dish, on top of the onion slices, bay leaf and 5 of the chestnuts. Sprinkle with Calvados. Add enough stock to come a quarter way up the quail. Cover with aluminium foil and bake for 25 minutes.

Remove the foil and bake for another 10 minutes.

Take the quail out of the oven and put them on a warm serving dish. Keep warm.

Strain the cooking liquid into a saucepan, pressing the vegetables to extract every last bit of juice and flavour. Reduce the liquid by boiling until it is quite syrupy. Add the remaining chestnuts and warm them through in the sauce.

Spoon the sauce over the quails and garnish with the chestnuts and chopped marjoram or other herb.

২ PASTA WITH CHESTNUT SAUCE

For those who own a pasta machine, here's a recipe for fettucini or spaghetti, but this sauce is also very tasty with store-bought pasta.

For the pasta:
300 g strong flour
2 tablespoons fresh basil, very finely chopped
1 clove of garlic
3 eggs

For the sauce:
30 g butter
200 g chestnuts, cooked and peeled
1 onion, sliced
4 spring onions, chopped
125 g sliced ham, cut into strips
120 ml single cream
2 tablespoons parsley, chopped
125 g grated mild cheddar cheese

Sift the flour into a bowl or the container of a food processor, add the basil, garlic and eggs and mix into a smooth dough. Knead for 5 minutes by hand, or 1 minute in the food processor. Roll the dough through the pasta machine and cut it into fettucini or spaghetti. Leave lying flat on a flour-dusted surface while making the sauce.

Melt the butter and fry the chestnuts until they're golden brown. Add the onion, spring onions and ham and fry for another 2 minutes on low heat. Stir in the cream and let simmer for 3 minutes until the sauce has thickened somewhat. Stir in the parsley and cheese and keep stirring until the cheese has melted. Season with salt and pepper.

Cook the pasta al dente (only about 2 minutes for fresh pasta; follow the instructions on the package if using store-bought pasta). Serve with the sauce on top and some extra grated cheese on the side.

🐌 LAMB WITH CHESTNUTS

This recipe comes from Claudia Roden's definitive *Book of Jewish Food*; it is a Turkish dish called *Hamim de kastanya*. It will serve from 6 to 8 people.

> *1 kilo boneless lamb (shoulder)*
> *1 large onion, chopped*
> *4 tablespoons sunflower oil*
> *salt, pepper*
> *1 ½ teaspoons ground cinnamon*
> *1 teaspoon ground allspice*
> *750 g chestnuts*
> *juice of half a lemon*
> *2-3 tablespoons chopped parsley*

Remove as much fat as possible from the meat and cut it in cubes of about 3 centimetres.

Heat the oil in a large enamelled pan with a lid and glaze the onion. Add the meat and brown it on all sides on medium heat.

Add the cinnamon, allspice, salt and pepper to the meat and mix well. Put the lid on the pan and simmer until the meat is tender, about 1 ½ – 2 hours.

In the meantime cook and peel the chestnuts

and add to the pan with the meat 15 minutes before dinner-time. Stir in a little lemon juice and sprinkle with parsley.

STUFFED PANCAKES

Because pancakes made with chestnut flour are rather heavy, I have kept the stuffing on the light side. For a lighter pancake, use the second batter below. As far as the mushrooms are concerned: here the wild mushroom lover can really come into his own – the wilder the better, and anything goes as far as varieties are concerned – my favourites being penny buns, hedgehogs and cauliflower fungus, which have a wonderfully nutty flavour that goes well with chestnuts.

> Batter 1:
> *300 g chestnut flour*
> *3 eggs*
> *1 pinch each salt and sugar*
> *50 g butter, melted*
> *750–1000 ml milk*

Batter 2:
160 g white flour
160 g chestnut flour
2 eggs
salt
40 g butter, melted
1 teaspoon oil
300 ml milk
300 ml water

Filling:
350 g mushrooms
50 g shallots
30 g butter
salt, pepper, Herbes de Provence (a mixture of
thyme, rosemary, marjoram, bay and fennel)
500 g fresh spinach
200 g cold cooked chicken (or turkey or guinea-fowl)
80 g crème frâiche

To make the pancakes sift the chestnut and/or white flour into a bowl and make a little crater in the middle. Break the eggs into it and sprinkle the seasoning on top. Add the melted butter and oil. Mix well with a fork or wooden spoon, adding the milk little by little, until it is a smooth batter. If it's too thick, add a little more milk. Chestnut flour has a tendency to clot, so make sure you smooth out all the lumps. Make your pancakes as thin as possible and set them aside between two plates while making the filling.

Clean the mushrooms with a damp cloth or brush and fry them with the chopped shallots in butter until they are lightly browned. Add salt, pepper and herbs.

Rinse the spinach, let it drain and cook it without adding any water in a large pan until is has just wilted. Put it in a colander and press out any excess liquid.

Cut the chicken into cubes and mix with the mushrooms and spinach. Add the cream.

Put a couple of spoonfuls in the middle of each pancake and fold them carefully. Pancakes made with only chestnut flour tear very easily!

Put the stuffed pancakes in a buttered oven dish, brush with some melted butter and sprinkle with some more Provençal herbs. Heat them through in a preheated oven at 200° C.

Accompanied by a fresh green salad, this is a very satisfying meal.

VEAL WITH CHESTNUTS

750 g veal (boneless, cubed, for stewing)
vegetable oil
2 tablespoons flour
salt, pepper
bouquet garni (thyme, rosemary, marjoram, tied up
in a bay leaf)
1 stalk celery, diced
12 small onions
500 g chestnuts, cooked and peeled
2 egg yolks
3 tablespoons dry white wine
½ cup double cream
juice of 1 lemon

Brown the meat in the hot oil, while sprinkling it with flour. Keep stirring, until the meat is well-covered. Douse with a little water, scrape the pan and season the meat with salt and pepper.

Add celery and bouquet garni and let it all simmer on low heat for half an hour with the lid on the pan.

Add the chestnuts and onions to the meat in the pan and let everything stew for another 45 minutes, uncovered.

Stir the wine into the beaten egg yolks and add cream and lemon juice. Stir this gently into the pan with the meat. Don't let it boil, otherwise the eggs will scramble.

Serve immediately with plain rice.

❧ GUINEA-FOWL WITH CABBAGE AND CHESTNUTS

The French name for this bird is 'pintade', referring to the verb 'to paint', in honour of its artistic feathers.

olive oil
1 guinea-fowl, cut into four or eight pieces
2 leeks, rinsed and coarsely chopped
3 carrots, scraped and coarsely chopped
2 onions, chopped
100 g unsmoked streaky bacon, in cubes
salt, pepper
10 Savoy cabbage leaves
parsley, chopped
30 chestnuts, cooked and peeled
150 ml stock (use chicken or veal, or of course guinea-fowl)

Heat a little olive oil in a large, heavy stewing pan and brown the pieces of guinea-fowl. Lower the heat and add the leeks, carrots and onions, parsley, bacon and seasoning and let them soften for a few minutes.

Add the cabbage and the stock and stew, covered, for about 40 minutes.

Add the chestnuts and correct the seasoning. Simmer for another 30 minutes. Serve with boiled potatoes dressed with some parsley butter.

BREAD, CAKES AND DESSERTS WITH CHESTNUT FLOUR

Because chestnut flour is rather sweet and heavy, it is often mixed with a little regular wheat flour. While researching this book, I came across many references (by French chefs) to the apparently delectable combination of chestnut bread and *fruits de mer*, shellfish, so there must be something in it!

CHESTNUT BREAD

600 g wheat flour
250 g chestnut flour
1 sachet hydrolized yeast, such as Harvest Gold
approx. 400 ml tepid water
15 g salt

Blend the flours together; mix in the yeast. Make a hollow in the centre and pour in the water. Mix with your hands into a dough. When this clings tidily together, bring it out of the bowl onto a flour-dusted worktop and knead for 10 minutes. Then add the salt and knead for 5 minutes more.

Leave the dough in the bowl, covered with a piece of oiled clingfilm or a cloth, to rise for an hour somewhere quite warm. Then divide it into two round loaves, or four smaller ones if you prefer. Put these on a buttered oven tray and leave them in the same warm spot to rise again for an hour and a half. Once more, cover the loaves with oiled clingfilm or a doubled teacloth so that they do not skin over. They should roughly double in size.

When you think they are ready, slash them with a cross on the top of each loaf and bake in a hot oven (220° C) for about 15 minutes. When they are done, they should sound hollow when tapping the bottom.

CHESTNUT POLENTA

A beautiful, dark polenta, to be enjoyed with a little goat's cheese, or pungent Italian *pecorino*, made with ewe's milk, to set off the sweetness. In Corsica, where chestnut flour is still much used, they call it *pulenda*. It can also be eaten with spicy sausages, or any number of tasty accompaniments.

1 litre water, or half water, half milk
500 g chestnut flour
salt
sunflower oil

In a large saucepan, bring the liquid to the boil then pour in the chestnut flour in a steady stream, stirring all the while. Season with salt. Continue to cook, stirring vigorously, until the mixture comes away from the sides of the pan.

Turn this dough onto a floured tea towel and leave to cool for a few minutes. Then roll it out into a disc-shape and let it rest a further 15 minutes.

Cut it into wedges, using a knife, or an oiled thread or cheese-wire if you want to do as the Romans do, and fry these in hot oil. Drain any excess oil by resting on kitchen paper, and serve hot.

❧ CASTAGNACCIO

In Castelpoggio, the mountain village in the Apuanian Alps where we worked one spring and summer, Spanish chestnuts and the white flour (farina dolce) *they produce when ground provided for centuries a basic diet. Polenta was made of chestnut flour and* castagnaccio, *a kind of rustic torta which has the consistency of a pudding and the aspect of a shallow cake. It used to be made in round shallow copper and brass pans, which were set in the ashes of the fire. In the last war, chestnuts and fungi and weeds were the only form of nourishment, unless the Castelpoggians undertook dangerous expeditions across the mountains, on foot, to Parma, a four day tramp often under fire, to barter their chestnut flour and salt for cheese and oil. Some people went on making this cake, baking it in the village bread oven, others preferred to forget it.*

PATIENCE GRAY, *Honey from a Weed*

I have very little to add to the above, except: let's not forget it. Patience Gray gives a recipe with fennel seeds and Malaga raisins; in other regions they put in candied orange peel or walnuts, while I prefer to make it with rosemary and pine kernels, according to Pellegrino Artusi's recipe in *Science in the kitchen and the art of eating well*.

> *500 g chestnut flour*
> *pinch of salt*
> *800 ml milk (or water)*
> *handful pine nuts*
> *1 tablespoon rosemary leaves, preferably fresh*
> *approx. 1 tablespoon olive oil*

Sift the flour into a bowl and add the salt. Gradually pour in the milk or water and keep stirring until all the lumps have disappeared.

Add the pine nuts and rosemary and mix well.

Pour some olive oil in a flat cake tin or earthenware dish, in which the cake will be about an inch thick, and pour in the batter. Dribble a little more oil on top and some pine nuts and rosemary and bake in a medium hot oven (190° C) for about half an hour, until firm, but not dry in the middle.

Remove the cake from the tin while still warm.

APPLE AND CHESTNUT *CLAFOUTIS*

This recipe was one of five supplied with my chestnut flour, bought in a French supermarket. A *clafoutis* is something between a thick pancake and a regular cake.

> *2 apples, such as Golden Delicious*
> *grated rind of a lemon*
> *100 g chestnut flour*
> *2 eggs*
> *1 tablespoon sugar*
> *250 ml milk*

Put the peeled, cored and sliced apples in a thickly buttered oven dish and sprinkle the lemon rind on top.

Mix the flour and the eggs and add sugar and milk.

Pour the batter over the apples and bake first for 15 minutes at 250° C, then turn the oven down to 175° C and bake for another 15 minutes, until lightly browned.

🐦 CHESTNUT CAKE WITH WALNUTS

> *8 heaped tablespoons chestnut flour*
> *2 tablespoons wheat flour*
> *2 teaspoons baking powder*
> *1 pinch salt*
> *4 eggs*
> *150 g sugar*
> *5 tablespoons oil (corn or sunflower)*
> *5 tablespoons milk*
> *100 g walnuts, shelled and broken*
> *100 g dark chocolate*
> *butter to grease the cake tin with*

Sift both flours and baking powder with the salt into a mixing bowl.

In another bowl beat the eggs with the sugar, the oil and the milk. Mix well.

Stir the egg mixture into the flour and mix until it is a smooth batter. Add the walnut pieces.

Put the dough into a buttered spring-form (a cake tin with a removable rim) and bake for about half an hour in a hot oven (220° C).

Melt the chocolate in a little water and glaze the cake with it.

🐦 CHESTNUT SHORTBREAD

50 g sugar
salt
1 egg
grated rind of 1 lemon (or orange)
200 g chestnut flour
100 g butter, in cubes
flaked almonds and 1 egg yolk

Put the sugar in a bowl with a pinch of salt, the egg and the lemon and mix well with a wooden spoon.

Add the sifted flour in one go and stir until the dough is crumbly.

Make a crater in the middle and put in the cubed butter. Knead until you have a smooth dough. Shape it in to a ball and let it rest for a few minutes.

Roll out the dough on a floured surface to a thickness of about 5 millimetres.

Preheat the oven to 220° C. With the use of a biscuit cutter, a jar lid or your hands, cut out round biscuits and put them on a buttered oven tray.

Brush with beaten egg yolk and decorate with slivers of almond.

Bake for 10 to 15 minutes until nicely browned.

BREAD, CAKES AND DESSERTS WITH WHOLE CHESTNUTS

෪ CHESTNUT BREAD

This bread can be made with dried, tinned or vacuum-packed chestnuts, so it may be enjoyed all year round; if you use dried ones, however, remember that they have to soak for a whole night before cooking. The recipe is from *French Country Kitchen*, one of Geraldene Holt's instructive and handsome books and she recommends eating it with *saucisson sec* or *jambon cru*.

> *225 g dried (or tinned or vacuum-packed) chestnuts*
> *2 teaspoons dried yeast*
> *150 g strong white flour*
> *225 g wholewheat flour*
> *1 tablespoon salt*
> *olive oil or butter*

If using dried chestnuts, soak them overnight and cook them in the same water for 45 minutes until they are tender. Leave them to cool in their cooking liquid.

Transfer the chestnuts to a food processor. Add some of the cooking water and reserve the rest.

Purée the chestnuts until smooth but still grainy.

Sprinkle the dried yeast on 150 ml warm water in a small bowl; leave for 10 minutes until foamy.

In a mixing bowl, stir the white and wholemeal flour with the salt. Add the chestnut purée, the yeast and sufficient of the chestnut cooking water to make a soft dough. Knead the dough on a floured board for 3 minutes and return to the bowl. Cover with a large plastic bag and allow to double in volume. This takes 1-2 hours in a warm room, or overnight in a cool room.

Knead the dough again for 1-2 minutes. Divide in four and shape each piece into an oval loaf. Place on a greased and floured baking sheet and make a shallow cut down the centre of each loaf. Set aside to prove (covered with oiled clingfilm or a doubled tea towel) for 30 minutes.

Bake the bread in a hot oven (220° C) for about 45 minutes or until each loaf sounds hollow when tapped underneath.

BASIC RECIPE FOR CRÈME AND PURÉE DE MARRON

The house of Clément Faugier, which since its establishment in 1882 has cornered the market for *marrons glacés*, at one point had the brilliant idea to use up the bits and pieces of broken chestnuts in the form of a paste, available sweetened and flavoured with vanilla or unsweetened in tins of various sizes. With this cream as a base a whole range of different recipes can be made.

PURÉE DE MARRON

Ideal to use in soups, soufflés, stuffings or flans and such, this paste can also be made with dried chestnuts, which you have to first soak overnight.

The ingredients are: cooked chestnuts, cream, butter, salt and pepper.

Purée the chestnuts in the food processor or in a vegetable mill (*mouli-légumes*) with the fine plate.

Put the purée in a pan and add cream in the proportion of 150 ml to 1 kilo of chestnuts. Warm it through on a low heat, stirring the while.

Add 50 g of butter and season with salt and pepper.

If the purée is too thick, add a little more cream or cooking water from the chestnuts.

🪱 A SWEET PURÉE DE MARRONS

Add the following ingredients to 500 g of unsweetened purée and beat well:

½ cup sugar
1 teaspoon vanilla extract
¼ teaspoon salt
2 tablespoons brandy
1 cup double cream

🪱 MONT BLANC

One of the simplest, most elegant of puddings: a
sweet, very thick chestnut purée is squeezed through
an implement with holes – a potato masher or a
mouli-légumes onto individual dessert plates. Cover
the peaks with freshly whipped cream, to which
you've added a tot of your favourite tipple, rum,
eau-de-vie, orange liqueur, brandy: *voilà*, everyone
his own mini-Mont Blanc!

🐚 MONET'S CHESTNUT COOKIES

The painter Monet is said to have been very fond of chestnuts and to have instructed his cook, Marguerite, to make these *galettes* regularly at tea time. This makes 18 cookies.

> *125 g butter*
> *1 cup unsweetened chestnut purée*
> *125 g light brown sugar*
> *3 eggs, separated*
> *1 teaspoon vanilla extract*
> *30 g chopped walnuts or hazelnuts (optional)*

In a saucepan, melt the butter over low heat, then add the chestnut purée, sugar, egg yolks and vanilla, stirring constantly. Heat through but do not boil. Remove from the heat and let cool.

In a mixing bowl, beat the egg whites until they form stiff peaks, then fold them with a spatula into the chestnut mixture.

Grease muffin tins and pour the batter into the moulds (filling the unused ones, if any, with water when baking).

Top with nuts if desired and bake in a hot oven (220° C) for about 20 minutes.

❧ DRUNKEN CHESTNUTS

A good way to preserve chestnuts: there is something primal and earthy about fruits and nuts in liquor, which were so often depicted in still-lifes during the 16th and 17th centuries; one feels warm just thinking about them.

Armagnac, brandy, grappa *or* eau-de-vie
1 kg chestnuts, cooked and peeled

for the syrup:
250 g sugar
1 glass water
1 vanilla bean (or a few twigs of aromatic herbs from the garden such as rue, verbena or sweet woodruff)

Put the chestnuts in a large stoneware or glazed pot or jar. It should have a well-fitting lid or a decent cork. Make the syrup by stirring the sugar into the water over medium heat until it dissolves; add the aromatics; boil steadily for 5 minutes. Allow to cool.

Pour the syrup over the chestnuts and top the jar with liquor. Shake well and let macerate for 3 months before use.

❧ CHESTNUTS IN MARSALA 1

Less strong than the above, and they require less *patience gastronomique* before they can be enjoyed. A nice dessert, warm or cold, with a little double cream.

115 g sugar
250 ml red wine
250 ml Marsala
500 g chestnuts, cooked and peeled

Put the sugar, red wine and Marsala in a saucepan, stir to dissolve, and boil for 5 minutes on low heat.

Carefully put the chestnuts in the liquid and boil together for another 5 minutes. Shake the pan from time to time, to make sure the chestnuts don't stick to the bottom.

Remove the chestnuts from the liquid with a slotted spoon and put them in a dessert bowl or ice-cream *coupe*. Boil down the syrup a little more and pour it over.

❧ CHESTNUTS IN MARSALA 2

Put cooked, peeled chestnuts in a dish and sprinkle sugar over them. Warm some Marsala in a ladle over the gas flame and set alight. Pour over the chestnuts while still flaming.

❧ CHESTNUT TART

> *1 egg*
> *250 g sugar*
> *250 g flour*
> *125 g butter, softened*
> *225 g* crème fraîche
> *250–300 g chestnuts, cooked and peeled*
> *ground cinnamon*

Make the dough by first beating the egg with 125 g sugar and then stirring in the flour. Knead the butter into the dough until it becomes smooth. Let rest for 25 minutes.

In the meantime beat the remaining 125 g of sugar with the cream and add a little cinnamon.

Roll out the dough and line a buttered baking tin with it. Pour in the cream and arrange the chestnuts in it in a nice pattern. Sprinkle with some more cinnamon.

Bake the tart for half an hour in an oven preheated to 200° C).

🐌 CHESTNUT-NUTMEG TART

This recipe is supplied by a chestnut farm in the United States.

Nutmeg pastry:
1 cup of flour
¾ teaspoon freshly grated nutmeg
1 tablespoon icing sugar
60 g cold butter, cut into cubes
1 egg yolk

Filling:
400 g cooked chestnuts, coarsely chopped
2 eggs, beaten
⅓ cup sugar
¾ cup light honey
2 teaspoons brandy
30 g butter, melted
grated rind of 1 small orange and 1 lemon
60 g dark chocolate, melted

Sift the flour, the icing sugar and the nutmeg in a mixing bowl and rub in the butter cubes until the mixture resembles a crumble topping.

Add the egg yolk and 1 or 2 tablespoons of cold

water. Mix well and shape into a ball. Wrap in plastic and put in the refrigerator for half an hour.

Roll out the dough and line a spring-form cake tin with it.

Put all the other ingredients, apart from the chocolate, in a bowl and mix thoroughly. Put the mixture in the spring-form with the dough and bake the tart in a medium hot oven (180° C) for about 35 minutes, or until golden brown.

Leave to cool in the tin and dribble with warm chocolate when unmoulded.

MARRONS GLACÉS

Now we are going to show M. Faugier that we can make our own glazed chestnuts. Especially for people who don't live at a stone's throw from a delicatessen, it will be nice to make this treat at home. In this case you have to buy or gather fresh chestnuts, and pick out the fattest!

1 kg chestnuts
1 kg icing sugar
300 ml water
vanilla extract
300 g caster sugar

Cook and peel the chestnuts as described in the previous chapter. Remove both skins carefully, so the chestnuts do not break.

Make a syrup with the icing sugar and 300 ml water, adding 1 teaspoon vanilla extract.

Put the chestnuts in this syrup and let them simmer over a very low fire for 30 minutes. Turn off the heat until the next day when the process is repeated: allowing the chestnuts to simmer gently in the syrup for a further 15 minutes. It is possible, but not usually necessary, to repeat this routine on a third day, and even more days than that, until the chestnuts have absorbed as much syrup as they can.

Now you can remove the chestnuts with a slotted spoon. With the caster sugar and a little of the cooking syrup, make a thick mixture and roll the chestnuts in it one by one, until they are coated with a layer of sugar.

They can be eaten after a day, and be kept for a month in the refrigerator.

Bibliography

In addition to those works cited in the acknowledgements, I have consulted the following:

Baker, Margaret, *The Folklore of Plants*, Shire Ltd, 2001.

Bentley, James, *Life and Food in the Dordogne*, Weidenfeld & Nicolson, 1986

Blanc, Suzanne and Henri, *La Châtaigne, Trésor d'Automne*, La Roche Beaumont, 1995

Canet, Michèle, *Recettes de Châtaignes*, Institut d'Études Occitanes, 1997

Castelvetro, Giacomo, translated by Gillian Riley, *The Fruits, Herbs and Vegetables of Italy*, Viking, 1989

David, Elizabeth, *French Provincial Cooking*, Penguin, 1970

———, *Italian Food*, Penguin, 1966

Edwards, John, *The Roman Cookery of Apicius*, Random House, 1993

Graham, Peter, *Mourjou: The Life and Food of an Auvergne Village*, Penguin, 1999

Phillips, Roger, *Wild Food*, Pan Books, 1983

Sauvezon, Robert and Antoinette, and Christian Sunt, *Châtaignes et Châtaigniers*, Edisud, 2000

There are also some useful internet websites which supplied me with a lot of information, notably: J. Hill Craddock at <http://www.utc.edu/Faculty/Hill-Craddock/chestnutlinks.html> and Allen Creek Farm at <http://www.ChestnutsOnline.com>.

Acknowledgements

I am very grateful to Claudia Roden for permission to cite a recipe from *The Book of Jewish Food*, Viking, 1997, and to Geraldene Holt for permission to use a recipe from her *French Country Kitchen*, Penguin, 1987. I thank the estate of Patience Gray for permission to quote from her *Honey from a Weed*, Prospect, 1986. I am also grateful to Keith Floyd for permission to quote from *Out of the Frying Pan, An Autobiography*, Harper Collins, 2000. I have also depended on the following books for quotations:

Dickinson, Emily, *Collected Poems*, Faber, 1991.

Goethe, J.W. von, *Gedichte.*

Heine, Heinrich, *De mooiste van Heine*, Atlas/Lannoo, Amsterdam, 1998 (tr. RL).

Herbert, Zbigniew, *Wiersze Wybrane*, Wydanictwo a5, Krákow, 2004 (tr. Alissa Valles).

La Fontaine, Jean de, *Fables*, Gallimard, Alfred Mame et Fils, 1888.

Lawrence, D.H., *Sons and Lovers*, Penguin, 1969.

Milton, John, *Gardens of Delight*, ed: Miles and John Hadfield, Cassell, London, 1964

Neruda, Pablo, *Odas elementales*, Cátedra, 1999 (tr. RL).

Roth, Joseph, *Die Geschichte von der 1002 Nacht*, Verlag Allert de Lange, Amsterdam, 1981 (tr. RL).

Stevenson, R.L., *Travels with a Donkey*, J.M. Dent, 1996.

Thomas, Edward, *Selected Poems*, Faber, 1984.

Thoreau, Henry David, *The Dispersion of Seeds*, W.W. Norton & Co, London, 2000.

Index